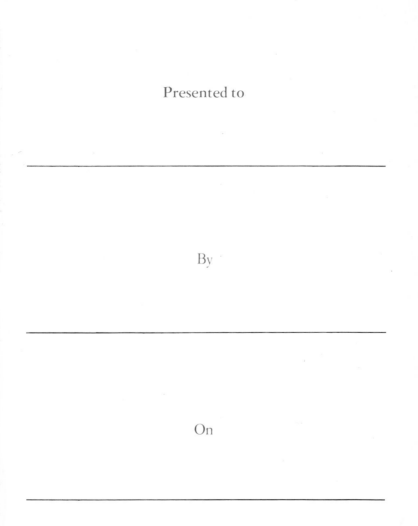

Presented to

_____

By

_____

On

_____

Ehrlich

The Life of JESUS

Edited by
LOUIS M. SAVARY

Illustrations by
RITA GOODWILL

Cover illustration by
GEORGE ANGELINI

THE REGINA PRESS
New York

1984
THE REGINA PRESS
7 Midland Avenue
Hicksville, N.Y. 11802

Illustrations © Copyright 1984 by H. Proost & Cie p.v.b.a. Turnhout, Belgium.

Cover illustration © Copyright 1984 by The Regina Press

ISBN: 0-88271-099-0

Printed in Belgium

FOREWORD

My dear child:

The life of Jesus is the greatest story ever told.

Jesus is the Son of God. He came to show us the way to Heaven. He taught us to love God and all our brothers and sisters.

The story of Jesus began almost 2000 years ago. It will not be finished until all of us have found our way to God the Father.

May Jesus bless you and always be your best friend.

The Editor

TABLE OF CONTENTS

THE LIFE OF JESUS

A VERY SPECIAL BABY

Many years ago, a very special baby was born in Bethlehem. His mother Mary held him and loved him and wrapped him in a blanket. Then she laid him down in a manger. They were staying in a stable because they could find no rooms in the village inn.

Mary's husband Joseph stood nearby. He was very happy to see the new baby.

Christians believe that Mary's baby is the Son of God.

SHEPHERDS CAME TO VISIT

Soon after the baby was born, some shepherds came to visit him, because they had seen angels during the night.

One angel said, "I'm going to tell you joyful news. Today is a great day for everybody because the savior of the world has just been born."

The angel told the shepherds the baby would be wrapped warmly, lying asleep in a manger. They went looking for the baby, and that's just how they found him.

A CHILD NAMED JESUS

When the baby was eight days old, he had a naming ceremony. Mary and Joseph gave him the name Jesus.

Then they took Jesus to the temple in Jerusalem to present their baby to God.

Simeon, a very old holy man, happened to be in the temple that day. When he saw Jesus, he took the child in his arms and began calling him "Savior of the world." Jesus looked like every other baby, but God told Simeon this baby was different.

EVERYONE WAS WAITING

That same day in the temple, a very old woman named Anna saw Simeon holding the baby Jesus. She loved God very much and He gave her the gift of seeing into the future. Without anyone telling her a word, she recognized Jesus as the Savior.

Anna came over and began praising God. And she began to tell people that the Savior everyone was waiting for had come.

Then Mary and Joseph took Jesus home.

A STAR POINTED THE WAY

Some wise old men also came to visit the baby Jesus. They came riding camels from lands far away. A star in the sky pointed their way to Jesus.

The wise men were happy to find Jesus. They brought gifts for the new baby—gold, frankincense and myrrh. These were gifts for a king. Even though Jesus did not look like a king, they knew he was one.

Then the travelers went back home to their own country.

JEALOUS KING HEROD

When the wise men first came through Jerusalem, they stopped at King Herod's palace. They said they were looking for the new-born Savior.

Herod seemed nice to the wise men. He told them to come back and tell him where the baby was so he could bring a present too. But secretly he was jealous. He didn't want anyone in his kingdom to have power or greatness.

So he ordered his soldiers to murder every baby under two years old that they could find.

ESCAPE IN THE NIGHT

The night before Herod sent his soldiers, Joseph had a dream. In his dream, an angel warned him. "Get out of bed right now and hurry to Egypt with the baby and his mother. And stay there until I tell you to come back. King Herod is going to try to kill the child."

So Joseph woke Mary, and with Jesus they set out for Egypt while it was still dark.

The next morning, Herod's soldiers came and killed all the other babies. But Jesus was safe.

IN A STRANGE COUNTRY

Egypt was a far-away country. It was a strange country, too. Mary and Joseph had no friends there. The Egyptians dressed differently. They spoke a language that Mary and Joseph didn't understand.

Joseph waited for the angel to tell them it was all right to go back home to Israel. They wanted to show Jesus to all their friends and relatives.

Finally, one night the angel appeared in Joseph's dream and told him to leave Egypt and return home.

WISE FOR HIS AGE

The town where they finally brought Jesus was called Nazareth.

Joseph was a carpenter, so he was able to build a house for his family. Mary took care of the house.

She and Joseph taught Jesus how to read and write. Jesus liked to read and write, and was quick to learn many things. People remarked how wise Jesus was for his age.

Mary and Joseph also taught him about how God loved the Jewish people. They told him about the holy city.

IN THE HOLY CITY

When Jesus was twelve, he was allowed to go to Jerusalem for the Passover feast. People from Nazareth went there together.

At the festival, men and women had different things to do. So sometimes Jesus stayed with his mother; other times he stayed with his father.

He saw the big temple, the priests and teachers. For the first time, he saw the crowds and felt the excitement and heard the noise of a big city.

JESUS IS LOST

Mary and Joseph lost Jesus in Jerusalem. They searched everywhere for him. After three days, somebody told them there was a young boy in the temple asking questions even the teachers couldn't answer.

Mary and Joseph hurried to the temple and found Jesus among the teachers, discussing the bible.

As they traveled home to Nazareth together, Mary and Joseph wondered about this special child of theirs.

LEARNING THE BIBLE

Back in Nazareth, Jesus helped his father in the carpenter shop. He was a hard worker, and everyone in the village liked him.

After work each day, time was set aside for learning the bible. Mary and Joseph told Jesus all the bible stories they knew. And Jesus would study the bible whenever he could.

Each Sabbath day, Jesus went to the synagogue. There, old men would read stories from the bible and explain them.

Jesus never seemed to hear enough about God.

HIS COUSIN JOHN

One of Jesus' cousins was named John. He would later be called John the Baptist. His family lived in the next town. The two boys were just about the same age. Often John and Jesus played together and talked together. They probably visited each other's homes for days at a time.

Both of them loved God very much and often talked about what God would want them to do when they grew up. Both of them wanted to serve God.

AFTER JOSEPH DIED

When Jesus was grown up, Joseph died. After Joseph died, Jesus had to earn a living and support his mother. Jesus was a fine carpenter. He was almost thirty years old.

Then, he heard that his cousin John was traveling from town to town along the River Jordan, baptizing people and telling them the Savior was coming soon.

And Jesus knew that the time had come for him to leave home and do the work of God.

A BEAUTIFUL WHITE CLOAK

One day Jesus told his mother, "I must go and do my Father's work."

But she already knew, without his saying it, that he would be going from Nazareth soon. For many weeks before, she had been weaving him a large white cloak to wear. It was a beautiful cloak, made all in one piece, without a seam.

One morning, dressed in his new cloak, Jesus said goodbye to his mother and he went off in search of John the Baptist.

THIS IS MY SON

Jesus stood among the crowd by the River Jordan one day. People were asking John the Baptist if he was the Savior.

John said, "No, I'm not the Savior, but he is coming soon."

Then Jesus stepped into the river and asked John to baptize him. When John poured water over Jesus, a dove flew down on Jesus. Then John heard God's voice saying, "This is my son. I love him very much."

And John realized for sure that Jesus, his cousin, was the Savior everyone was waiting for.

JOHN THE APOSTLE

John was a follower of John the Baptist. He was very young. He was one of the first to meet Jesus. The Baptist introduced them to each other.

John visited the place where Jesus lived, and when Jesus asked John to join him, he was happy to do so.

John was very special to Jesus. They often sat next to each other at dinner. John is called "the Apostle whom Jesus loved."

THE APOSTLES

Some of John's followers came to Jesus and asked if they could join him. He said, "Yes."

These men went and told others to come and see Jesus. "He is the one we have been waiting for," they said. Soon Jesus was accompanied by many people.

One day, Jesus chose twelve men to be his special followers. These men were called the Apostles. From now on they would stay with him always.

WONDERFUL WINE

Jesus and the Apostles were invited to a wedding. His mother Mary was there, too.

Mary noticed that the wine supply was running out and told Jesus. Jesus called the waiters and told them to fill six big waterpots full of water. Then he said, "Dip some out and take it to the head-waiter."

"This is delicious wine," the headwaiter said. And this was the first miracle that Jesus performed.

MATTHEW

One day while Matthew was sitting at his tax collector's booth, Jesus passed by. He looked into the booth at the young man and said, "Come, be my follower." Matthew jumped to his feet and walked along with the other Apostles.

That night Matthew had a big dinner at his home to introduce his friends to Jesus. After that, Matthew left the tax business and became a companion of Jesus.

TOO MANY FISH

Once Jesus got into Peter's boat and told him to go out into the lake to catch some fish.

Peter said, "We've been fishing all night and didn't catch a single fish. But if you say so, we'll try again."

Then as soon as they threw their fishing nets over the side, so many fish swam in that the nets were full and almost broke.

After that miracle, Peter followed Jesus and never left him.

TIME FOR SUPPER

One day, Jesus and his followers were going to Peter's house. Peter had invited everyone for supper. When they arrived at the house, Peter's mother-in-law was sick in bed with a high fever. She was supposed to do the cooking.

So Jesus went over to her and touched her hand. That's all he did, and she got better so fast that she was able to get out of bed and have everything ready in time for supper.

FROM TOWN TO TOWN

With his Apostles, Jesus went from town to town.

In each place he would teach all day, telling people about the kingdom of God. Everybody loved to hear Jesus talk.

After speaking, he would ask people who were sick to come to him. And he healed them — the sick, the lame, the blind, the insane. The crowds were a-mazed when he would heal people by saying a word or touching them.

As news spread of his miracles, the crowds that followed Jesus grew bigger and bigger.

NOT AFRAID OF LEPERS

Suddenly the crowd stopped. "A leper is coming," someone cried.

A leper is somebody with a skin sickness. People were afraid of lepers, so nobody went near them. But Jesus wasn't afraid. He went up to the sick man and asked what he wanted.

"Sir," the leper said, "if you want to, you can heal me."

"I want to," Jesus answered. "Be healed." Instantly all the sickness disappeared. The crowd was amazed.

A PARALYZED BOY

A Roman army officer came to Jesus and said, "A boy who works for me is paralyzed and full of pain. Please come home and heal him."

"Yes," said Jesus. "I will come."

Then the officer said, "Sir, you don't have to come. I know that even right here, if you tell the boy's sickness to go away—it will go."

"Go along home," Jesus said. And when the officer got home, he found the boy cured.

THROUGH THE ROOF

Four men carrying a stretcher arrived outside a crowded house. They brought a friend who was paralyzed. They wanted Jesus to heal him, but there was no way to get in.

So they dug through the clay roof. And when the hole was big enough, they lowered their paralyzed friend by ropes right in front of Jesus.

Jesus healed the sick man. Next day, everybody helped repair the roof they had broken.

STRETCH YOUR ARM

One sabbath in synagogue, Jesus noticed a man with a deformed arm. He was ashamed of it and kept it hidden.

Some people would be angry at Jesus if he did a miracle now, because that would be doing work on the sabbath, which wasn't allowed.

But Jesus said that helping people is more important, so he told the sick man, "Stretch out your arm."

When the man stretched out his arm, it became normal just like the other one.

ONLY SLEEPING

"My little daughter has just died," a rabbi cried to Jesus, "but you can bring her back to life again."

When Jesus arrived at the rabbi's home, people were weeping loudly as the funeral music was played.

Jesus said, "Please ask everyone to leave. The little girl isn't dead, she's only sleeping."

People sneered at him. "We know when somebody is dead," they said.

Then Jesus took the girl by the hand and she awoke and was alive again.

SUDDENLY THEY COULD SEE

One day, two blind men followed Jesus, holding each other's hands and using their sticks to find the way.

Jesus asked them, "Do you believe that I can make you see?"

"Yes, we do," they told him.

Then he touched their eyes and said, "Because you believe, it will happen."

And suddenly they could see. They looked at one another and laughed and hugged. Their joy knew no bounds.

ALL ALONE IN THE WORLD

A funeral procession carried a young boy who had died. At the village gate, Jesus saw the boy's mother. She was walking next to the coffin and crying. She was a widow and had no other living relative. She was all alone in the world.

Jesus told her, "Don't cry." Then he walked over to the coffin and said, "Young man, come back to life again."

And the boy sat up and began to talk. And Jesus gave him back to his mother.

TO TOUCH HIS COAT

Jesus was walking along, the crowds all around him. A woman who wanted to be healed came beside him and touched his coat.

She had been sick for twelve years and could find no cure. She had tried every doctor in town and had spent all her money on medicines they told her to take. But the instant she touched Jesus' coat, her sickness stopped.

Jesus blessed her. "Go in peace," he said.

FOOD FOR EVERYONE

One day Jesus was teaching in the countryside.

At night, the crowd was still there, and they had nothing to eat. There were over 5,000 people. One boy had five loaves of bread and two fishes. Jesus blessed the loaves and fishes and gave them to his followers and said, "Feed everybody."

Then the food kept multiplying until there was enough for all. And there were lots of leftovers, too.

JESUS LIKED TO PRAY

One of the most important things that Jesus taught people was that God loved them and would answer their prayers.

Once the Apostles asked Jesus how they should pray to God. And Jesus taught them The Lord's Prayer.

Often, Jesus would pray for many hours. He prayed to God his Father in heaven. "God is everybody's Father," he said.

Jesus told everybody to pray often because God was pleased when people spoke to him.

A TERRIBLE STORM

Jesus said to his friends, "Let's go in our boat and cross the lake." That day Jesus was so tired, he fell asleep in the back of the boat.

Next came a heavy rainstorm. The Apostles were afraid the boat would sink and they would all drown. "Help!" they shouted to Jesus.

Then Jesus spoke to the wind and the sea. "Quiet down," he said. And the wind stopped, and the sea became calm.

A WILD MAN

A wild man lived in a cemetery like an animal. People chained him, but he would break the chains as if they were pieces of string. Nothing was strong enough to control him.

When this man came up to Jesus, he fell down in front of him. He was afraid of Jesus.

"Come out of this man, you evil spirits," said Jesus, talking to the demons who lived inside the wild man, tormenting him. And the wild man then became a normal, human being.

NOW I CAN SEE

People brought a blind man to Jesus. First, he wet the man's eyes and then laid his hands over them. "Can you see anything now?" Jesus asked.

The man looked around, "Yes," he said, "I can see people over there, but not very clearly. They look like tree trunks walking around."

So Jesus put his hands over the blind man's eyes again until his eyes were perfect. "I can see everything well now," said the blind man. "How can I ever thank you?"

THE BENT-OVER WOMAN

While Jesus was speaking, he noticed a woman who was bent over double. She couldn't stand straight or even raise her head. She could only look down. And she had been this way for eighteen years.

Jesus called her over to where he was standing. Then he touched her and she was able to stand up straight, just like everyone else.

She was happy beyond words.

SITTING BY THE ROAD

When a blind beggar heard the crowd, he began to shout, "Jesus, have mercy on me."

"Shut up," some people yelled at him.

But the blind man shouted all the louder, "Jesus, have mercy on me!"

Soon, his shouting caught everyone's attention and Jesus said, "Tell him to come here."

So they said to the beggar, "You lucky man. He's calling you. Come on."

"I want to see," the blind man begged Jesus. And instantly, Jesus cured him and he was able to see.

MARTHA, MARY AND LAZARUS

Martha and Mary were sisters. With their brother Lazarus they lived in a big house outside of Jerusalem. Whenever Jesus and his Apostles came to Jerusalem, they would stay at Lazarus' house.

Having dinner in their house and speaking with them was enjoyable for Jesus. Friends make you feel at home, and that's what Martha, Mary and Lazarus did for Jesus.

LAZARUS COME OUT

One day, Jesus received a message that Lazarus his friend was very, very sick. By the time Jesus arrived, Lazarus had died and was buried in a cave.

When they showed him the cave where Lazarus was buried, Jesus began to weep, for he loved Lazarus very much.

Then he ordered the stone in front of the cave rolled aside. And in a loud voice, Jesus shouted, "Lazarus, come out!" And Lazarus came out. A dead man was alive again.

THE BIGGEST MIRACLE

In Jerusalem, Jesus had a lot of enemies who wanted to kill him. And Jesus told his followers, "They will put me to death, but in three days I will rise up again."

Then on the day people call Good Friday, his enemies had Jesus put to death. After he died, his friends buried him in a tomb.

But on Sunday morning, as he promised, Jesus came out of the tomb by his own power. He was alive. And many followers saw him.

It was the biggest miracle ever.

THOMAS

Thomas the Apostle liked to ask questions, and when he didn't know something, he asked.

Thomas was also brave. He was ready to march into Jerusalem and face death with Jesus.

When Jesus rose from the dead and appeared to the Apostles, Thomas wasn't with them. When they told Thomas, he said, "I don't believe it." But Jesus came again so that his friend Thomas could see with his own eyes. And Thomas believed.

THE PROMISE OF JESUS

Jesus died when he was still a young man. Some people hated him and had him put to death.

But that is not the end of Jesus' story, because he came back from the dead. On Easter Sunday morning, Jesus came out of his grave alive.

He visited with his Apostles and friends for over a month. Then he said goodby and ascended into heaven.

Jesus promised that one day all of us will live together with him and his Father forever.

PRINTED IN BELGIUM BY

proost
INTERNATIONAL BOOK PRODUCTION